The Three Billy Goats Gruff

by Barrie Wade

Illustrated by Nicola Evans

FRANKLIN WATTS
LONDON • SYDNEY

Once upon a time, there were three Billy Goats Gruff.

The three Billy Goats
Gruff were very hungry.

Sweet grass grew in the meadow on the other side of the river ...

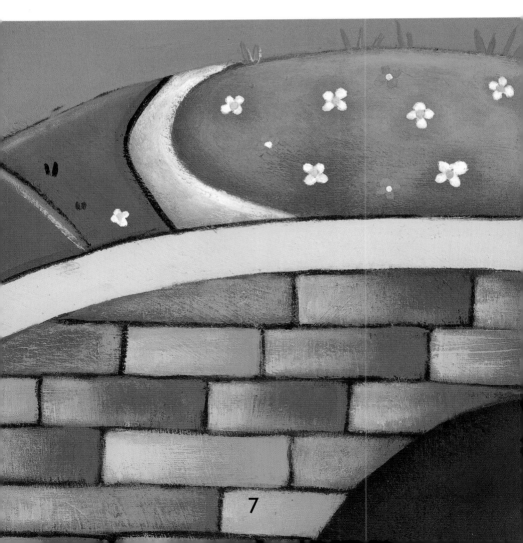

... but a wicked old troll
lived under the bridge.

The littlest Billy Goat Gruff
clattered onto the bridge.

"Who's that trip-trapping across my bridge?" the troll roared.

"It's only me!" squeaked the littlest Billy Goat Gruff.

"I'm going to eat you up!"
roared the wicked troll.

"But my brother is much fatter than me," said the littlest Billy Goat.

"Really?" said the troll, and he let the littlest Billy Goat cross his bridge.

Then, the middle-sized
Billy Goat clattered onto
the bridge.

"Who's that trip-trapping across my bridge?" the troll roared.

"It's only me!" said the middle-sized Billy Goat.

"I'm going to eat you up!"
roared the wicked troll.

"But my brother is even fatter than me," said the middle-sized Billy Goat.

"Really?" said the troll, and he let the middle-sized Billy Goat cross his bridge.

Then, the biggest Billy Goat clattered onto the bridge.

"Who's that trip-trapping across my bridge?" roared the wicked troll.

"ME!" bellowed the biggest Billy Goat Gruff.

"I'm going to eat you up!"
roared the wicked troll.

"Oh no, you're not!"
the biggest Billy Goat
roared back.

"Oh yes, I am!" roared
the troll.

26

The biggest Billy Goat
Gruff snorted, put down
his head and charged.

He butted the troll up into the air, right off the bridge and into the river.

The wicked old troll was never seen again.

The three Billy Goats
Gruff ate the sweet grass
in the meadow ...

... and lived happily
ever after.

Leapfrog has been specially designed to fit the requirements of the National Literacy Strategy. It offers real books for beginning readers by top authors and illustrators.

There are 31 Leapfrog stories to choose from:

The Bossy Cockerel
Written by Margaret Nash, illustrated by Elisabeth Moseng

Bill's Baggy Trousers
Written by Susan Gates, illustrated by Anni Axworthy

Mr Spotty's Potty
Written by Hilary Robinson, illustrated by Peter Utton

Little Joe's Big Race
Written by Andy Blackford, illustrated by Tim Archbold

The Little Star
Written by Deborah Nash, illustrated by Richard Morgan

The Cheeky Monkey
Written by Anne Cassidy, illustrated by Lisa Smith

Selfish Sophie
Written by Damian Kelleher, illustrated by Georgie Birkett

Recycled!
Written by Jillian Powell, illustrated by Amanda Wood

Felix on the Move
Written by Maeve Friel, illustrated by Beccy Blake

Pippa and Poppa
Written by Anne Cassidy, illustrated by Philip Norman

Jack's Party
Written by Ann Bryant, illustrated by Claire Henley

The Best Snowman
Written by Margaret Nash, illustrated by Jörg Saupe

Eight Enormous Elephants
Written by Penny Dolan, illustrated by Leo Broadley

Mary and the Fairy
Written by Penny Dolan, illustrated by Deborah Allwright

The Crying Princess
Written by Anne Cassidy, illustrated by Colin Paine

Jasper and Jess
Written by Anne Cassidy, illustrated by François Hall

The Lazy Scarecrow
Written by Jillian Powell, illustrated by Jayne Coughlin

The Naughty Puppy
Written by Jillian Powell, illustrated by Summer Durantz

Freddie's Fears
Written by Hilary Robinson, illustrated by Ross Collins

Cinderella
Written by Barrie Wade, illustrated by Julie Monks

The Three Little Pigs
Written by Maggie Moore, illustrated by Rob Hefferan

Jack and the Beanstalk
Written by Maggie Moore, illustrated by Steve Cox

The Three Billy Goats Gruff
Written by Barrie Wade, illustrated by Nicola Evans

Goldilocks and the Three Bears
Written by Barrie Wade, illustrated by Kristina Stephenson

Little Red Riding Hood
Written by Maggie Moore, illustrated by Paula Knight

Rapunzel
Written by Hilary Robinson, illustrated by Martin Impey

Snow White
Written by Anne Cassidy, illustrated by Melanie Sharp

The Emperor's New Clothes
Written by Karen Wallace, illustrated by François Hall

The Pied Piper of Hamelin
Written by Anne Adeney, illustrated by Jan Lewis

Hansel and Gretel
Written by Penny Dolan, illustrated by Graham Philpot

The Sleeping Beauty
Written by Margaret Nash, illustrated by Barbara Vagnozzi